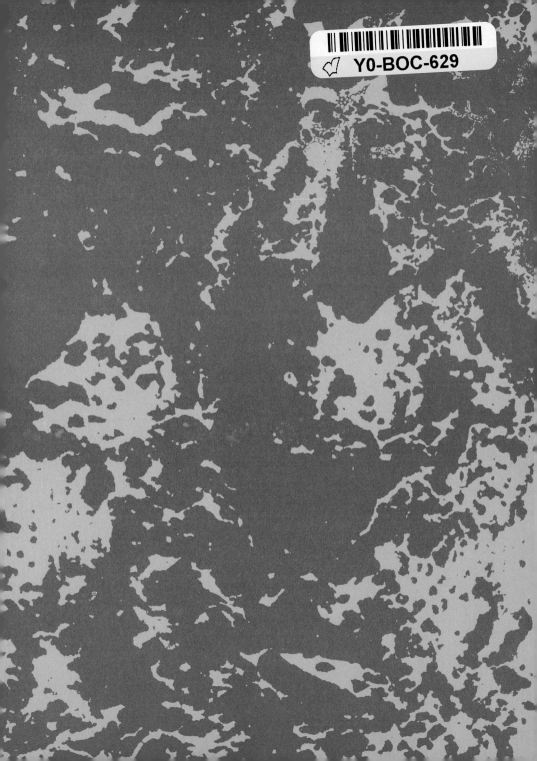

Nuggets

OF WISDOM
AND FOLLY

BY RALPH WOODS

JACKET PHOTOGRAPH
BY ALAN FONTAINE

PUBLISHED BY
THE C.R. GIBSON COMPANY
NORWALK, CONNECTICUT

Contents

I. Poetic Justice 5
Just rewards and fair exchanges

II. Mysteries and Misdeeds 10
Sins that come to light unexpectedly

III. Wile and Trickery 14
Using your head, turning-the-tables and changing the rules

IV. Incentives and Success 18
Sizing-up the situation, salesmanship and profitable schemes

V. Fools and Misfortune 24
Slips-of-the-tongue, poor judgment and comical mishaps

VI. Lessons From Life 29
Ultimate questions, truths and tales of human nature

VII. The Baffling and Bizarre 34
Unaccountable incidents and extraordinary events

I. Poetic Justice

THE BEST INTENTIONS

A widow of high social position, but reduced circumstances, lived alone in quiet dignity. One day she received an invitation to the wedding of the daughter of old friends of great wealth and the most lofty social eminence.

Realizing she could not begin to match the magnificent gifts others would send the bride, she decided to search second-hand shops and pawn shops in the hope of encountering some unusual trifle at a price she could afford to pay.

Finally she encountered four prices of matching china which her instincts and cultivated taste told her were genuine antiques and obviously once part of a valuable set. The price was within her means so she bought the pieces and sent them to the bride's home with her card, trusting that the modest nature of her gift would be overlooked in the opulent profusion of other wedding gifts.

When the wedding gifts were displayed, the gentle old lady was relieved to notice that her gift was missing from the glittering array.

As she turned to leave the room, she saw the demure pieces of china on a separate table near the door, and with it a card reading: "For years our family has searched for these specific pieces of china to complete a set handed down through many generations. Our deepest appreciation to Mrs. Bradbury Lonsdale for such priceless treasures."

"THE BEST LAID SCHEMES____"

A young man, despondent because of unrequited love, decided to end it all on a cliff overlooking the Pacific Ocean. Determined that his resolution should not miscarry, he took with him a rope, a pistol and a bottle of poison. He fastened the rope around his neck and the other end of it to a tree. Then he stepped to the edge of the cliff, swallowed the poison, and as he leaped into space, he fired the gun at his head.

The bullet missed his head but cut the rope. When he dropped into the sea the salt water he swallowed made him vomit the poison. And since he was a good swimmer he naturally struck out for the shore.

MEASURE FOR MEASURE

A wealthy man presented a mink coat to a beautiful young matron with whom he visited when her husband was out of town on frequent business trips. The matron was delighted with the gift, but wondered how she might accept it without arousing her husband's suspicions. The wealthy donor of the coat suggested that she put the mink in an old suitcase of his, check it at the railroad station, and then come home and say she had found a checkroom ticket on the street or bus.

The matron did this and then asked her husband to pick up whatever was checked, on the off-chance it might be something valuable. After mild protests, the husband finally agreed to stop at the railroad station checkroom on his way home from work and claim whatever the ticket called for.

When the husband received the valise, he opened it in an obscure corner of the station and discovered the new mink coat. He removed the coat from the valise, presented it to a young woman friend, went to a second-hand clothing store and bought some cheap odds and ends and brought the valise home to his excited wife. "Nothing in it," he said, "but a bunch of rags. I told you this morning it wouldn't be worth the trouble."

A BIG RETURN

A clothing manufacturer found himself with a staggering inventory of fur-lined coats when style changes made them obsolete. He thought he could at least cut his losses by billing twenty of his best accounts for a dozen coats each, and then shipping each account thirteen of the coats. He depended upon the cupidity of the retailers to assure acceptance of the shipments.

His customers' cupidity, however, was matched by their resourcefulness. Every one of the twenty accounts returned twelve coats for credit.

LOOK BEFORE YOU SPEAK

A lawyer successfully handled a difficult law case for a wealthy friend.

Following the happy outcome of the case; the friend and client called on the lawyer, expressed appreciation of his work, and handed him a handsome Moroccan leather wallet.

The lawyer looked at the wallet in astonishment and handed it back with a sharp reminder that it could not possibly compensate him for his services. "My fee for that work," acidly snapped the attorney, "is five hundred dollars."

The client opened the wallet, removed from it a one-thousand-dollar bill, replaced it with a five-hundred-dollar bill, and handed it back to the lawyer with a smile.

A FAIR EXCHANGE

Prior to World War I Lord Kitchener, Commander-in-Chief of the British Armies, called on a distinguished Indian rajah. Toward the end of a pleasant visit the rajah asked if there was anything in his possession that the General would like to have. Kitchener noticed a steel and ivory sabre that hung on the wall, and said he would like to have it. "Alas!" exclaimed the rajah, "it is the one thing I could not surrender since it has been in my family for hundreds of years."

Soon thereafter the rajah called on Kitchener, and he in turn was asked if there was anything in Kitchener's possession he would like to have. The rajah pointed to an Oriental vase, but Kitchener said he could not part with it. The vase, also, had been a family heirloom for hundreds of years.

Some years later Kitchener met the rajah and said that he could, after all, have the desired Oriental vase. The rajah reciprocated by offering Kitchener the sabre. When the exchange was made examination revealed that both articles had been manufactured in Birmingham, England.

UNAWARE OF ANGELS

It was the year 1884. A middle-aged couple of quite ordinary appearance called on Charles Eliot, president of Harvard University, introduced themselves and said they had just returned from Europe where their son had suddenly become ill and died.

"We won't take too much of your time," said the woman, who missed nothing. "We just want to talk about a memorial to our son—something that would help young men to get an education."

Eliot looked at the unprepossessing couple with impatience and a suggestion of aristocratic disdain.

"Perhaps you have in mind a scholarship?" said Eliot crisply.

"No," said the couple. "We have in mind something more substantial than that; perhaps a new building or so."

"I must explain to you," said Eliot with what seemed a patronizing air, "that what you suggest costs a great deal of money. Buildings are very expensive."

The lady arose and said, "President Eliot, what has this entire university cost?"

Eliot muttered something about several million dollars.

"Oh, we can do better than that," said the now decisive lady. "Come, Leland, I have an idea." And they left.

Some time later President Eliot of Harvard learned that the unpretentious couple he had treated so cavalierly had contributed twenty-six million dollars for a memorial to their son—to be named Leland Stanford, Jr, University.

THE STRANGE BARGAIN

A one-year-old Cadillac was offered for sale in a newspaper advertisement at a price of $50.00. Most people thought it was an error or a joke, but one man decided to inquire. He went to the address given, a luxurious estate. He was met by a quiet, middle-aged woman, who verified the accuracy of the ad and showed him the car. It was in perfect condition and drove beautifully. The man quickly paid the woman $50 and took delivery of the car.

Then the buyer asked the woman why she sold him for $50 a car that was obviously worth thousands of dollars.

"It's quite simple," said the lady. "My husband died last week and his will provides that the proceeds from the sale of his Cadillac must go to his young secretary."

AN EXECUTIVE DECISION

The chief executive of a large corporation, who was a stickler for efficiency, made an inspection tour of one of the company's manufacturing units. As he led his aides from department to department, he glowed with satisfaction as machines hummed and men worked swiftly and capably.

Suddenly the ears of the chief executive were annoyed by the sound of whistling coming from behind a partition. He swung in the direction of the sound and quickly confronted the whistler, a young man sprawled lazily on a chair.

"What's your salary?" demanded the chief executive.

"Who, me?" asked the whistler.

"Yes, you."

"Thirty-five bucks a week," replied the young man before he resumed whistling.

Wheeling on his retinue, the chief executive snapped, "Give this boy two weeks pay and get him out of here at once."

"But, C.E. . . . " began a particularly courageous assistant.

"You heard me—seventy dollars and out," interrupted the chief executive as he strode away.

Later that day an accounting department officer brought up the subject of the whistler.

"To what account shall we charge that seventy dollars, C.E?"

"Pay-roll, naturally," was the official answer.

"But, C.E., that boy didn't work for us. He was a messenger waiting for a delivery receipt."

II. Mysteries and Misdeeds

THE FOOLISH PARISHIONERS

The parishioners of a village in the grape-growing region of California decided to honor the fiftieth year in the priesthood of their beloved pastor. Times were bad and cash was scarce, so they decided that each person would bring a gallon of wine and pour it into the padre's almost empty wine barrel.

When the appointed Sunday came each parishioner arrived with a gallon jug and poured the contents into the pastor's wine barrel. After Mass a delegation of parishoners called on the good father and told him what they had done. The old man was delighted and insisted that they all repair to the wine barrel and drink a glass in honor of the occasion.

But when the "wine" was drawn it was found to be water. Each thrifty parishioner, thinking no one else would have the same idea or notice the difference, had brought a gallon of water instead of the promised gallon of wine.

ICED EVIDENCE

Two rival scientists were exploring the frozen and barren regions of the Arctic Circle. After one day-long expedition, one man returned to base, explaining his companion had fallen into a deep ice crevasse.

Some time passed and then suddenly the survivor was indicted, tried and convicted of murdering his campanion.

The only evidence presented at the trial was an account of the discovery of the perfectly preserved body of the dead man. It was frozen upright in an iceberg that drifted south in the spring and into the shipping lanes. A bullet had penetrated the man's temple—as easily and clearly seen as if the crime had been committed a few hours previously.

THE MAN WHO TOLD THE TRUTH

American Jews were justly proud in 1906 when President Theodore Roosevelt appointed Oscar Straus to his Cabinet as U.S. Secretary of Commerce and Labor.

Shortly thereafter a private dinner was given to celebrate the event, attended by the President. In explaining his selection, the President told the diners that Mr. Straus was chosen for his character and ability, without regard to race, creed, color or party. "And", added Mr. Roosevelt, "Jacob Schiff will confirm the fact that I sought only the best qualified man for the post."

Mr. Schiff, presiding at the celebration—wealthy, respected, gently senescent and quite deaf—nodded and said, "Dot's right, Mr. President, I remember you said to me, 'Chake, who is the best Jew I can appoint as Secretary of Commerce?' "

THE THRIFTY KILLER

A Chicago businessman and his wife took a plane for a destination in the foothills of the Rocky Mountains, where they planned to spend two weeks mountain climbing. Three days after their arrival a broken-hearted husband came back alone to their Colorado hotel and told how his wife had slipped and fallen over a cliff. A search party found the mangled body. The place from which she fell was notably precarious, so the husband was quickly cleared at the inquest which followed.

The story of the tragedy was printed in the Chicago papers, accompanied by a picture of the couple. Shortly after, the husband was arrested, tried and convicted of murdering his wife. A ticket agent who had sold the husband the plane tickets testified that he had asked for a one-way ticket and one round-trip ticket.

THE LETHAL PACKAGE

A woman left her pet cat in an animal hospital for treatment, but several days later it died. In order to assure the animal a fitting burial, the woman had the veterinarian place the remains in a neatly wrapped cardboard box, which she picked up.

On her way home from the animal hospital the woman stopped in a large department store to do some shopping. While examining some articles, the woman placed the box on an adjoining counter. A few moments later she discovered it was missing.

The loss was immediately reported to store detectives. A short time later they found the box on the floor of a telephone booth, with the cover off and the dead cat's face leering grotesquely at the beholder. Alongside the box was the body of a woman, identified by store detectives as a professional shoplifter. Apparently she had taken the box to a telephone booth to examine its contents. The sight of the dead cat so shocked her that it caused a fatal heart attack.

ONE GRIM REMINDER

A poor and middle-aged Mexican named Pablo grew weary and vexed with the care of his very old and feeble father. Finally he secretly told his son to take his ailing grandfather to a remote stretch of barren land and leave him there, with a little food and a blanket so that the end would not be too pitiful for the old man.

When the boy returned he carried half of the blanket.

"Why did you bring back that piece of blanket?" asked the irate father.

"I'm saving it for you," said the boy.

SOLID EVIDENCE

In the gold-mining region of Ontario, Canada, the authorities were troubled by the theft of partly refined gold by employees of the mining and smelter companies. Although the Mining Act forbids the operation of a smelter without a license, the thieves refined the gold in home smelters undetected because they only worked late on cold nights when the light blue smoke and sulphurous odor of gold cooking is not easily discovered.

But one illegal operator was exposed hours *after* he had finished cooking his gold. He had cooked partly refined gold stolen from a mining company which used mercury in its process. It had been a bitterly cold night. The mercury went up the chimney with the smoke, but the cold solidified the mercury and it settled on the roof of the man's house.

The next morning everyone in town, including the police, discovered what had been going on the previous night. The once black roof of the man's house now shone like silver in the sunlight.

UNREASONABLE DOUBT

The defense lawyer in a murder trial recognized that the outcome of his case depended chiefly upon instilling in the jury a " reasonable doubt" of guilt. During his summation, the defense attorney reminded the jury that if they had any reasonable doubt, they were bound to acquit his client charged with murder.

"You have heard it testified that a dismembered arm and leg were those of the allegedly murdered victim. Allegedly, I repeat. For in exactly ten seconds the supposed victim of this supposed murder is going to walk through that door and into this court room!"

The defense lawyer counted slowly and dramatically to ten, while wide-eyed jurors, attorneys, spectators, court attendants and judge stared at the door. The door did not open.

"You see, gentlemen," the lawyer said trimphantly. "You have proved my point. You watched the door expecting to see the allegedly murdered man walk into this court room. Therefore you do have a reasonable doubt that the man was murdered. I rest my case, asking you to acquit my client."

The jury, however, returned a verdict of "Guilty."

After the jury was dismissed, a newspaper man asked the foreman why the jury was not impressed by the defense's illustration of "reasonable doubt."

"It was a clever stunt," replied the jury foreman, "but I and two other jurors watched the defendant when the lawyer was counting.

"The defendant never once glanced at the door. He knew the man was dead, because he murdered him and had no doubt about it."

III. Wile and Trickery

AN IDENTIFIABLE SOURCE

During the Stalin regime in Russia, it was the practice of the Soviet Foreign Office to issue its statements for foreign correspondents at about 3 a.m. The usual custom was to notify the correspondents to be at the Foreign Office about midnight, and then to keep them waiting for hours in the rain, snow and bitter cold. They would then be admitted into the building and instructed to walk up several floors where the Foreign Minister or his assistant would hand them the bulletin. They always saw either the Foreign Minister or his next-in-charge.

One cold night, however, after an unusually long wait outside, the correspondents were not allowed to enter the building but instead were handed a bulletin by the building superintendent who told them that the Foreign Minister told him to distribute it.

One American that night began his story with these words: "According to a bulletin issued by the janitor of the Soviet Foreign Office—".

After that day, all the foreign correspondents were invited into the building immediately upon their arrival.

THE PARKING VIOLATION

In a hasty, thoughtless moment a man left his car parked for several hours in front of a fire hydrant on a non-parking street. It was also facing the wrong way on a one-way street. When he returned to his car he found it had been tagged by the police with tickets for nearly one hundred dollars in fines—a sum he could by no means afford.

So the man boarded a bus, rode some few miles away and phoned the police that his car had been stolen from the location at which he was phoning. The police told him to relax and they would check into the situation. Within an hour the police phoned back that the car had been found. They did not mention the parking tickets which were voided in view of their belief that the car was illegally parked by the thief.

UNMITIGATED TRUTH

The first mate on a ship got drunk for the first time in his life. The ship's captain, a stern and rigid man, recorded in his log for that day. "The first mate got drunk today."

The mate protested against the entry, explaining that if it remained in the log without further comment or explanation, it would suggest that drunkenness was not unusual for him and could affect his career. The captain, however, was adamant, stating that the log recorded the exact truth and therefore must stand as written.

The next week it was the mate's turn to write the ship's log. And on each day he wrote down these words:

"The Captain was sober today."

A TIMELY RETRACTION

One day, a woman writer of a syndicated gossip column included a series of racy items that reflected on the morals of an actor who was unusually sensitive to such comment. The actor phoned the columnist, denied the truth of the items and demanded a retraction. The columnist was curt and uncooperative.

The actor warned her that if she persisted in assailing his reputation he would prove that even her spotless reputation was not immune to mud-slinging.

That evening, and for five succeeding nights, the actor parked his flashy and custom-built convertible with its familiar low-number license plates, in front of the columnist's home on a main road. The car was kept parked throughout each night.

On the seventh day the woman's column contained an unqualified retraction of the disparaging items followed by a tribute to the actor's high moral character and fine reputation.

THE SUCCESSFUL MISTAKE

An agitated man called on his attorney and told him that he had loaned five hundred dollars to an acquaintance, but had failed to get any written acknowledgment of the debt. "And," added the client, "when I asked him for his note or I.O.U. he became very angry. Now I am afraid he plans to ignore the debt. If only I had something in writing, I could sue him if he refuses to repay the loan."

"Leave it with me," replied the lawyer. "I think I can get something in writing from him. Stop in some day next week and we'll talk about it some more."

When the client again called on his lawyer he asked, "How did you make out?"

"Just fine. I've got a letter from him. It was easy. I wrote asking that he drop me a line stating he had borrowed one thousand dollars from you."

"But that's wrong. It wasn't a thousand dollars, only five hundred."

"I know," said the lawyer. "That's what he said in this letter. It's all the proof you need."

MAKING GOOD

A dentist spotted a deadbeat patient while dining at his country club one evening. He called the patient aside, reminded him that he owed him $250 for work done more than two years earlier, and insisted the man pay up. To the dentist's astonishment, the patient pulled a check book from his pocket and wrote a check to the dentist for the full amount.

Skeptical about the man's good faith, the dentist went directly to the bank the next morning and presented the check for payment. The teller handed back the check with the explanation that the patient's account was a little short of the amount of the check. Following a few minutes of good-natured conversation, the dentist learned that the man's account was twenty-five dollars short of the needed amount. The dentist smiled, went to the customers' desk for a few minutes, came back to the teller, and deposited thirty dollars to the account of his former patient. He again presented the $250 check and walked out with a net gain of $220.

JUST TOO CLEVER

The quick-tempered and very demanding head of a small business was planning to leave on an extended sales trip. Shortly before he set out, the plant's new night watchman went into the boss's office and asked him to postpone his trip.

"Why? And anyway what business is it of yours?"

"None, sir," answered the watchman, who was trying to gain favor. "But I had to come in and warn you. You see, last night I dreamed you would be killed in an accident if you went on this trip."

"You dreamed it, eh?"

"Yes, last night."

"In that case, get your pay and get out. You're fired!" shouted the boss who did not want a night watchman who slept on the job.

NOTHING NEW

The owner of a newspaper instructed his managing editor to hire the proprietor's son, just out of college, as a reporter. Rather than assign him to a news story at which he might fail, the editor promptly assigned the young man to cover a big society wedding.

Late in the day the managing editor came upon the new reporter deep in a mystery story.

"Where's the wedding story? It's almost press time," asked the editor.

"Oh, there's no story," said the reporter casually. "The whole thing blew up. The bride eloped last night with some local jerk—a drummer in a band, I think."

Hours later, after several aspirin, the editor decided on the young reporter's next assignment. He would wait patiently for the next war.

IV. Incentives and Success

THE LABEL COLLECTOR

A man who collected junk and sorted it out for whatever was saleable, began to save the labels from tin cans and bottles. He sorted these labels by brands, products and sections of the town. It interested him to discover the way consumer preferences varied according to neighborhoods and he learned a lot about various products.

Eventually, when the junk collector had enough money saved, his studies of labels enabled him to open a small grocery store in the most productive neighborhood and to stock it with precisely the products and brands the people in that section most preferred.

APPEAL TO VANITY

A prominent millionaire was sued for divorce. His wife named as corespondent a beautiful young woman of questionable reputation.

The newspapers carried the story but none of them had a picture of the allegedly beautiful corespondent. Shortly after the first editions were on the street the proprietor of one paper phoned his editor with the command: "Get that woman's picture—and I don't care how you do it."

The editor ordered every available man on the staff to work at securing the picture. Reporters disguised as telephone repair men, electric company meter readers, building inspectors, all gained entrance to the woman's house but none of them could get a picture. Her servants could not be bribed. Commercial photographers either had never taken her picture or refused to admit it.

In desperation the editor turned to a just-hired cub reporter. "Here, son," said the editor, "get me a photograph of this woman.

Here is her name and address. Just the picture—no interview necessary. And make it quick."

In less than an hour the young reporter was back in the office with the picture, a very fine one. He was bewildered by all the excitement it caused.

He started to speak to the editor. "Hold it," said the editor, "I want all the other men to hear you tell me how you got the picture."

When everyone had gathered the editor turned to the cub reporter and said, "Now tell us how you got that picture."

"Well," said the embarrassed young man, "I went to the address you gave me, rang the bell, asked the servant who opened the door if I could see Miss Glamor. When she came to the door, I told her where I was from and asked if she would give me a beautiful photograph of herself rather than run one as unflattering as those we usually take. She was delighted at my consideration and gave me her portrait."

AN OLD NEW ACT

A New York night club was not doing enough business, chiefly because it was not being mentioned in the newspapers, especially in the entertainment columns. The club's publicity man explained to the management that one of the surest ways to get press mention was for the club to introduce a new act. The management said that no new act would be engaged. So the publicity man invented one—an exotically named dance team doing spectacularly new dancing; a team newly arrived in the United States and making its American debut. Publicity releases were prepared about the new, but mythical dance team, and sent out to all the columnists.

During the next four or five days the columnists proved they read publicity releases. Every one, in his own characteristic patter, praised the dancers and the club for its enterprise. The night club's business picked up remarkably, although none of the columnists had been near it. And it didn't seem to make any difference to the customers that the great new dancers weren't better than the old dancers.

THE EXPERT

An important and complicated machine in a factory mysteriously stopped working. Machinists and engineers strove desperately to locate the trouble and correct it, but all failed. Meanwhile production in the plant had to be stopped until an expert could be called in to fix the all-important piece of equipment. The expert arrived, tinkered with the machine briefly, tapped here and there a few times with a hammer, and the machine resumed operation.

When the expert submitted his bill for $250 the plant manager was aghast, and said to him: "All you did was to tap the machine a few times. Please itemize your bill."

The expert took the bill and wrote at the bottom of it:
Tapping Machine With Hammer $1.00
Knowing Where to Tap $249.00

THE WOMAN WHO WAS TIPPED

A customer of a large department store complained to the management that the attendant in the ladies' room had stared coldly at her when she did not leave a tip.

"But we have no attendant in our ladies' room," insisted the manager.

When the customer replied indignantly that she was not in the habit of lying, the manager promised an investigation would be made. It was discovered that a matronly woman had wandered into the ladies' room for a rest. When she took out her knitting and sat there and relaxed, people began giving her coins. She simply went back each day with her knitting and continued to accept the gratuities handed to her.

THE CAT SELLER

An experienced antique fancier visited a shop in the hope of encountering an unsuspected bargain. While puttering around, she noticed a cat licking milk from an old saucer which she instantly recognized as an antique worth hundreds of dollars. But being wise in the ways of antique dealers, she went to the sleepy-eyed shopkeeper and said: "What a charming little cat you have. I love them, especially when they are as friendly as this one."

"Yes, it's a friendly animal," replied the dealer with disinterest.

"Could I buy it?"

"You want it? Well, it's my little girl's cat and it would upset her terribly if I sold it."

"I'll pay twenty-five dollars for it"

The shopkeeper finally relented and took the money.

As the woman started to leave with the cat in her arms, she stopped and said, "Oh, I forgot. If you don't mind I'll take this old saucer along, too. The cat apparently is used to it and might miss it."

"No," said the now alert shopkeeper. "I can't let you have the saucer."

"Why not? I'll pay you a few cents for it."

"No, it's not for sale."

"But why not—it's only a useless piece of crockery."

"You're wrong, madam. That old saucer is very valuable. I would not sell it for less than $700. Besides, I sell an awful lot of cats on account of that saucer."

THE SOUND OF GENIUS

During a concert given by the great Paganini, string after string of his violin snapped, until only one good one remained. The audience laughed its amusement over the artist's predicament.

Paganini, by no means amused, lifted his crippled instrument and said to his audience, "Now you will see what Paganini and one string can do."

And show them he did, by completing the performance with all notes of the concerto played on the single remaining string.

A HELPFUL SALES MANAGER

A young life insurance salesman walked into the office of an executive and said to him: "I am selling life insurance, but I don't suppose you would be interested."

The executive, sales manager for a thriving corporation, looked at the insurance man in disgust and belligerently said that he certainly did not want any life insurance from him.

"In that case," said the young salesman, "I suppose I will have to try someone else" and reluctantly started to leave.

"Wait a minute," said the sales manager. "I employ and train salesmen and I've seen some beauts in my day, but you are without doubt the worst I have ever met. You'll starve to death if you continue to talk people out of your product, instead of talking them into buying it." Whereupon the sales manager gave the young man a rapid-fire course in the technique of selling insurance. He got so interested in the whole problem that he ended up buying a $10,000 life policy for himself.

"Let this be a lesson to you," said the sales manager. "Work out a sales pitch for each individual situation you are likely to encounter and use it to the hilt."

"That is what I have been doing," smiled the young salesman.

"You see, I had you figured out before I came in here. So I used my specially prepared pitch for the aggressive sales manager."

SUPER SALESMAN

A retailer was overstocked with television sets at a time when new models were coming on the market. How to sell these suddenly out-dated sets was a serious problem.

Finally, the retailer hired a salesman and equipped him with a hearing aid. Then the boss moved his desk to a balcony overlooking the salesroom.

When a customer came in to look at television sets, the salesman would fiddle with his hearing aid and call up to the boss on the balcony: "How much is this set?"

The boss would lean over the railing and call down: "It's just been reduced; it's three hundred and forty dollars."

The clerk would look a little uncertain, nod to the customer, and fool with the hearing aid and then say: "It's two hundred forty-four dollars. I think that's what he said."

Before long all the old model television sets were sold. "There's a lesson in this," said the boss to the salesman, "you cannot cheat an honest man."

THE COMPETITORS

A peddler with a pushcart loaded with cheap socks parked at a busy corner in a poor neighborhood and hawked his wares in a loud voice. Some people looked but no one bought anything from him. Presently another peddler appeared on the scene with a load of cheap socks and in an even louder voice began to advertise his merchandise at prices lower than his competitor. The first peddler glared at the new arrival, berated him, and raised his cry an octave or two. The second peddler shouted back and then resumed calling out what a greater bargain he was offering.

Before very long the second peddler was doing a thriving business; in fact, all the business. After several hours he had sold his entire stock and happily departed. The other peddler sorrowfully pushed his burdened cart away.

Some blocks away the two peddlers met, did some calculating, exchanged money, had lunch together, loaded up the empty pushcart with more socks, and moved off to another neighborhood.

V. Fools and Misfortune

TEST OF TIME

As train-time neared an Erie railroad conductor was approached by a man he did not know, who said he was a fireman on the road and had to get to Elmira in a hurry. "I forgot my pass, but I'm sure it's all right with you." The conductor was reluctant to allow the man free transportation, but the stranger was persuasive and rather convincing; so the conductor relented, but with some misgiving.

When the train got under way the conductor passed down the aisle collecting tickets. When he came to the man who said he was a railroad fireman he greeted him cordially, and said "Say, my friend, have you the time on you?"

"Sure have," said the man as he reached for his watch. "It's exactly twenty minutes past nine."

"Oh, it is, is it? You're no railroad man—a railroad man wouldn't say 'twenty minutes past nine.' He'd say 'nine twenty'."

"Now you show your pass, pay your fare, or get off the train."

THE OVERSTATEMENT

There was once a bright young man who made himself valuable to his employer. He was clever, sharp and industrious and he rose quickly to a position of some importance in the concern. One day a friend convinced the young man that he was not being paid enough, considering how valuable he was to his employer. The youth was easily persuaded that he should demand a raise. The raise was readily granted to him.

After several months the youth decided that since the raise had been so willingly given him he should make additional demands on his employer. This too was given him by the boss, though not quite so readily.

A little later on the young fellow made a third demand for more money. The boss demurred.

"I know all about your business," the youth declared to his boss. "Either you'll pay me what I'm worth or I'll leave. You know you can't get along without me."

"Oh," said the boss, "that's a rather extravagant over-statement. What do you suppose we'd do if you died? Do you think we'd have to shut down?"

"Well," stammered the young man, "in that case I suppose you'd just have to get along."

"Then, in that case," concluded the boss, "You're fired! And from now on we'll consider you dead!"

THE JUDGE WHO BELIEVED IN EQUALITY

A judge in a rural area was presiding over a dispute concerning a large area of valuable grazing land that had an even more valuable mineral potential. Neither side was confident of either the legality or justice of its position. The attorneys involved in the case would not hazard any predictions as to which side the judge would favor.

On the second day of the trial the judge began the proceedings by making the following statement: "Gentlemen, I believe it will be agreed that I have always been fair and impartial in my decisions. And I intend to remain unswayed by anything except the evidence and the law. Now, last evening two envelopes were handed me. One contained four thousand dollars from one party in this case. The other contained five thousand dollars from the other party. But in order to remove any suspicion of influence I am returning one thousand dollars to the party who gave me five thousand dollars. That makes everything even. We will now go on with the case."

RICHES IN THE BIBLE

The young man was bored by work on the family farm, made uneasy by the hazards of agriculture, and attracted by accounts of the exciting life of the big cities. "I'm going to New York," he told his parents. "I have enough saved up to take care of myself until I get a job."

"That is a very unwise decision," declared his father. "If you think country life is bad, wait until you see what it is like in New York. Remember, don't ask us for money unless it is for train-fare home."

Just before the son left his home his mother handed him a small Bible with a metal clasp. "If you ever get discouraged or need help," she said, "promise me you will read Psalm 46. It will be of great help to you."

The father's warning proved true. The lad discovered that he was not equipped to fill the few job openings he heard of. Down to his last few cents he fell into conversation with a man who was hiring laborers for subway construction. He promised the young fellow work within three days. But the young man had no money for even two more days. So he wired home to Virginia for the train fare, and was met at the station by his parents.

Later that day he said to his mother: "It was a tough break. I had a job lined up but no money left for the week before I would get paid."

"Did you read the Bible I gave you?" asked his mother.

"Mother, please understand: I needed money, not religion."

The mother picked up the Bible, released the clasp, turned to Psalm 46 and showed him the fifty-dollar bill she had placed there for him before he left.

ADVICE OF COUNSEL

A law suit involving a large sum of money had been heard before a judge.

In the corridor outside the court-room the defendant, who was faced with financial ruin if the decision went against him, listened to his attorney.

"Well, it's up to the judge now, and frankly, I wouldn't attempt to read his mind."

"How about me sending the judge a box of cigars with my card," suggested the defendant eagerly.

"Good Lord, no!" snapped the attorney. "This judge is a stickler for ethical behavior. A stunt like that would prejudice him against you, and he would probably hold you in contempt of court. Don't even smile at him."

Several days later the judge rendered a decision in favor of the defendant.

As the defendant left the court house with his attorney he said, "Thanks for the tip about the cigars. It worked."

"I should say it did. We would surely have lost the case if you had sent them."

"But I did send them."

"You did?"

"Yes. That's why we won the case."

"I don't understand," said the puzzled attorney.

"It's simple. I sent the cigars to the judge and enclosed my opponent's card."

CAUGHT IN THE ACT

The boss noticed one day that his chief clerk was signing letters dictated earlier in the day without a glance at contents or address. The boss rebuked him and told him that he must read every letter carefully before signing it. The clerk agreed.

A serious stenographic error in a letter was not caught by the chief clerk. The boss was much more severe in his reprimand this time. The clerk insisted he was now reading every outgoing letter with great care. The boss said nothing more. He went back to his office and dictated a letter to his secretary and told her to type it and place it among the next batch of letters given the clerk for his signature.

The next day the clerk was called into the boss' office.

"I've received your letter, and I accept your resignation," said the boss.

"What's that, sir?" said the astonished clerk.

The boss handed him a letter.

The letter was addressed to the boss and signed by the chief clerk. It read: "In view of the fact that I am either unable or unwilling to obey your instructions, I hereby tender you my resignation, effective immediately."

THE ENRAGED COLLEGIANS

One of the more spectacular Notre Dame football teams had the experts puzzled at half-time of an important game when it trudged back to the dressing room, a badly whipped and bewildered aggregation of young men.

Yet, when the team returned to the field for the last half of the game, the young collegians played as though enraged, tearing through their opponents like inspired madmen, and winning the game by a wide margin. It was a surprising transformation from a first half lack-lustre team to a second half maniacal-rushing machine.

Between halves the team had sat morosely in the dressing room awaiting coach Knute Rockne and the inevitable thunder.

Shortly before time to go on the field for resumption of play, the door opened. Rockne stood at the threshold, glanced swiftly over the players, bowed gently but unsmiling, then turned and left as he said over his shoulder, "I beg your pardon, girls, I was hoping to find the Notre Dame football team."

A MADDENING SITUATION

A man got on a train at Buffalo early one evening and said to the sleeping-car porter: "I'm a sound sleeper, but I have got to get off at Albany. I've been elected to the State legislature and must be sworn in tomorrow morning. So be sure to wake me up. Force me off at Albany, even if I am still in my pajamas."

The porter promised to do as requested.

When he awoke, the newly-elected man found that he was in Grand Central Station, in New York City— a hundred miles away from Albany. And he was swearing and screaming at the top of his voice.

"What's the matter with that guy?" a trainman asked the porter, who was hiding behind a door. "He is sure mad."

"Yes, he's mad enough," said the porter. "But he's not half as mad as the guy I put off at Albany last night."

VI. Lessons From Life

THE ULTIMATE QUESTION

An English bishop relates that one day he was riding in a London bus when an elegantly dressed young man boarded it: pin-stripe trousers, opulent cravat, boutonniere, delicate breast pocket handkerchief, gloves held in a carefully manicured hand, bowler hat, tightly-rolled umbrella, and a face notable only for its blank expression.

The young man seated himself opposite a woman and a young boy. The boy inspected the fop carefully for a minute or two, then turned to his mother and in an embarrassingly high-pitched voice he asked:

"Mummy, what sort of man is he?"

The mother's reply was inaudible. But the boy's question lingered in the air, so that other people on the bus suddenly began to wonder about the dandy,—and about themselves, too.

SNAP JUDGMENT

A young woman boarded a railroad train, sat down next to an elderly lady and presently engaged her in conversation. She told her older companion that she was going to vist her ill mother, but that she could not stay long because finances were a bit difficult with them and her husband was able to give her only her railroad ticket and a twenty-dollar bill.

A little later the younger woman excused herself and went to the ladies room. While there she realized she had left her pocketbook on the train seat, but quickly dismissed her sudden fear when she recalled that the nice old lady would watch it until she got back.

Shortly after she returned to her seat the older woman excused herself and went to the ladies room. The young woman took advantage of the absence to check in her purse to be sure that her twenty-dollar bill was still there. It was gone. Thereupon she angrily took up the other woman's purse from the seat, opened it, found a twenty-dollar bill on the very top, took it, transferred it to her own purse, and made no comment about it to the older woman when she returned.

At the next stop the younger woman got off and went directly to her mother's home. Later in the day her husband phoned to tell her he found the twenty-dollar bill she had failed to take with her that morning.

THE POLITICIAN

A man running for State office on the 1940 Republican ticket did not hesitate publicly to state that he supported and favored the election of the Democrat, Franklin D. Roosevelt.

Members of the Republican County Committee called this man before them, pointed to his political inconsistency in running as a Republican while supporting a Democrat for the Presidency, and told him his conduct was embarrassing the party. "Make up your mind what you are right now," said the Republican leader of the county, "and tell us."

"I'll gladly tell you, gentlemen," replied the man who was challenged. "I am a politician."

THE MYSTERIOUS PRISONERS

Among the German prisoners of war brought to the United States and held in P.O.W. camps were two young men who puzzled both their fellow-prisoners and the American authorities who tried to question them. The German prisoners insisted they knew nothing about the mysterious men. They kept to themselves and talked to no one. The pair was frightened and bewildered, but not sullen. They seemed willing to cooperate, but no one could understand a word they said. Since they were Mongoloid in appearance, experts in Asiatic languages were called in. It was eventually established that the two prisoners were Tibetans. They were happy at long last to be able to tell their story.

In the summer of 1941 the two friends, goaded by an adventurous impulse to see something of the world, made their way across the northern frontier of Tibet and for weeks wandered in Soviet Russian territory. All of a sudden they were picked up and shipped off to they knew not where. They were given rifles, some rudimentary military training and quickly sent to the front to fight the Germans. Good Buddhists as they were, they were horrified at the idea of killing. The Germans took them prisoner and eventually put them into an auxiliary service of the German army occupying France. After the Normandy invasion, they were given guns and told to fight with the Germans. The Americans took them prisoner and shipped them with other prisoners across the ocean.

When they had finished their story, the interpreter asked them if they had any questions. They did. The one thing they wanted to know: "Why are all the people shooting at each other?"

THE PUZZLE SOLVER

A man sat struggling to complete some work he had brought home from the office, but his eight-year-old son kept interrupting him. Finally the exasperated father picked up a jig saw puzzle, scattered the pieces on the floor, and said, "Put this map puzzle together and stop bothering me."

Fifteen minutes later the young boy said, "Daddy, I've finished it!" The amazed father looked and found the boy had spoken the truth. "How did you ever do it so quickly?"

"Easy," smiled the boy. "On the other side of the map puzzle, there is a picture of a child. When you put the child together, then the world comes out all right."

THE MESSAGE

A ten-year-old orphaned girl had become a problem to the official of an orphanage. She wasn't naughty or a trouble-maker, but she was painfully shy, aloof and awkward. The head of the institution was proud of her unfailing success in handling morose and introspective children but this enigmatic child puzzled and eventually exasperated the Director and her matrons. Try as they would, they could not break through the child's extreme reserve, or tempt the child away from her wistful watching at the window of her second-floor room.

Finally, the orphanage official became so thoroughly annoyed at her failure to "reach" the child that she decided to watch the little girl for some act that would justify the orphan's transfer to a medical institution.

One bleak, drizzly day a matron discovered the little girl in the act of dropping a note out of the window to the bustling street below. Summoning the head of the orphanage to join her, the matron dashed to the street and triumphantly recovered the child's note. The two women stood in the street and read it, then silently hung their heads in shame. The note read:

"To whoever finds this—I love you."

TRAGIC TALENT

One day an elderly man called on Dante Gabriel Rossetti, famous nineteenth-century poet and artist, asked for his opinion of some sketches he showed. Did they have any value? Did they suggest he might eventually gain recognition as an artist?

The gentle Rossetti struggled to avoid speaking the truth to his visitor, but finally felt obliged to tell the old man that his work was without value and showed little or no promise.

The crushed caller then produced some additional sketches "done by a young art student."

Rossetti immediately enthused over the second group of sketches and declared that the young artist should be given every help and encouragement.

The old fellow was deeply moved. He shook his head and said, "Ah, I was that young artist!"

GUILTY CONSCIENCE

Advertising men, to illustrate the value of experts, tell about a man who lost a valuable umbrella and placed the following advertisement in the local paper:

"Lost from the local church last Sunday morning a silver-handled black umbrella, with MST engraved on it. The gentleman who took it will be well rewarded by leaving it at No. 10 Maple Street."

No umbrella was returned. The man mentioned this to a friend in the advertising business, who persuaded him to place a new advertisement in the paper, reading somewhat like this:

"If the man who was seen taking an expensive umbrella from the local Church last Sunday morning wishes to avoid public exposure and a blot upon his heretofore stainless Christian character, he will return the article at once to No. 10 Maple Street. He is well known."

The next day the missing umbrella was found on its owner's porch, along with eight other umbrellas, plus three that had been thrown on the front lawn.

VII. The Baffling and Bizarre

THE LESSON OF DARKNESS

To dramatize the fact that the dark teaches us lessons we do not learn at any other time, Cleland Boyd McAfee recalled to mind the sinking of the *Republic* one night in 1910 in the Atlantic.

The *Republic* became disabled during the afternoon in an unusually heavy fog. The *Baltic* was nearby and came promptly to the rescue, trying desperately to locate the sinking vessel, sailing round and round in the fog and blowing its whistle incessantly, but failing to sight the *Republic*. When night came those aboard the *Baltic* concluded it would be impossible to locate the other vessel until morning.

But they were wrong. When darkness descended, those on the *Baltic* saw the lights of the other vessel—the vessel that could not be seen in the murky light of the afternoon.

THE MYSTERIOUS FIGURE

One black midnight a special train carrying Queen Victoria was racing to make up time lost because of violent storms. Suddenly the engineer saw in the distant glare of the train's headlights the figure of a man standing in the middle of the tracks, frantically waving his hands. The brakes were jammed on, the train came to a grinding, lurching stop, spilling Her Royal Highness and members of her entourage into the aisles. The train crew leaped to the ground and rushed forward to see what was the matter. Two hundred feet ahead a bridge had been washed away by the storm. If the train had not been halted, the Queen and her distinguished fellow-passengers would certainly have perished.

A search was immediately made for the person who had so providentially flagged down the train. But he had mysteriously disappeared. Just when the search for the benefactor was being abandoned, one of the train crew cried out and pointed to a moth captured by the engine's headlights. The waving figure had been nothing more than an image on the snow of this tiny moth crazily dancing in the air closer and closer to the beam of light from the locomotive.

THE POWER OF SUGGESTION

Two amateur but irresponsible psychologists decided to try an experiment on a physically strong but impressionable young farm worker. Their aim was to make the sturdy lad ill through the power of suggestion. They began by separately inquiring, in anxious tones, about the worker's health. Having planted the seed of doubt by this kind of carefully spaced out questioning, the two experimenters then began to express outright concern about the young man's health, deploring how badly he was looking, asking if he felt run-down or had any persistent pain or strange sensations, and entreating him to take care of himself.

The consequence of this dangerous foolishness was that the completely healthy young fellow took to his bed with an illness the doctors could not identify or understand.

When the "psychologists" realized what they had done, they got busy to reverse the harm they had caused. They called frequently on the patient, observed he was looking better, gently scoffed at the ponderous comments of the doctors on the case, and gradually raised the young man's confidence in his condition to such an extent that before long he was back working on the farm in full vigor. And in his innocence, the fellow gratefully thanked his two new friends who had shown such concern for his welfare.

THE SENTENCE OF THE TONG

A newly-arrived Chinese man took up residence in the Chinatown of a large American city where his ignorance of the new land's language and customs would not prevent him from earning his living. He was happy to be in America and pleased to be among his own people in so strange a land. But the newcomer violated an important law of the powerful tong to which he belonged and he received a sentence of death. In deference to American laws, the tong issued a decree to all Chinatown stating that effective immediately, the man was to be considered dead. The tong took no other action beyond the issuance of this decree.

The object of the sentence laughed.

Chinatown elected not to hear his laugh nor his voice, nor did anyone seem to see him. He was dead by edict to every man, woman and child in Chinatown.

The victim soon began to realize that his situation was humorless. He had no home, no food, no possessions and no means of communication with anyone outside of Chinatown. Chinatown was the only world he knew and in it he was considered dead.

Rapidly the sentence of silence closed remorseless claws about his thinning throat. He went from hunger to horror to hopelessness, and one morning his body was found in the gutter.

The sentence of the tong had been legally executed.

THE LOVER'S BANQUET

In the early days of the New Orleans' Mardi Gras a handsome young man from the North was struck by the beauty of a girl with another group at the ball they were both attending. He kept staring at the girl until she looked his way. Instantly there was between them that silent communication experienced only by people suddenly stricken by love.

The man excused himself from his friend and walked quickly to a moon-bathed balcony. The beautiful young woman joined him a few minutes later, furtive and blushing.

"You are heartless," she said "to induce me to leave my fiance in this way. It's wrong."

"No," he replied, "We are compelled by love in youth and beauty."

They smiled uneasily and spoke briefly, and then the man urged her to join him in supper. She demurred saying it would endanger her reputation. He said in that event he would immediately marry her. So off they went to a certain famous restaurant and ordered the waiter to serve them as fine a meal as he could. For hours through the night they ate and sipped wine and talked of their lives, their hopes and plans for the future. As the dawn of Ash Wednesday appeared they went to the first Mass at St. Louis Cathedral and were then quietly married by one of the priests. The girl took her husband home to meet her family, who had worriedly searched the night for her.

A week later the happy couple left for the North, where several months later the girl died. Her husband never again returned to the Mardi Gras.

But a few days before the next Mardi Gras the restaurant where they had first dined received a generous check from the bereaved widower with the request that it be used to serve at the same table, the same meal the couple had eaten that memorable night. And every year at Mardi Gras time the restaurant received another check with the same request. The restaurant always complied, seriously serving the memorial dinner to the ghostly diners.

This continued for twenty years, when the restaurant received a letter from a New York law firm, stating that the widower had died and provided in his will for a trust fund for the continuation of the same dinner each year at Mardi Gras time as long as the restaurant was in business.

To this day at a certain New Orleans restaurant, on each Shrove Tuesday, a waiter carefully and quietly serves an elaborate meal for two phantom guests, at a gaily decorated table.

THE LAST WORD

Two college professors were bitter enemies. Their frequent and often brilliant arguments amused some members of the faculty, but tired others because each man insisted upon having the last word.

One of the professors, Smith, died in November, after a lingering illness. Jones, his opponent, was not disturbed by Smith's death. In March crocuses began to peep through the earth and Jones, from his study window, took pleasure in watching them struggle to maturity. But as they grew taller, Jones saw that they spelled out JONES IS A FOOL. The college chuckled at Smith's way of having the last word.

Not long thereafter Jones became mysteriously sick and was ill for some time. Eventually he recovered and resumed teaching. Ten years later he died. He left his entire estate to the college, including his body to the medical school. His will specified that his body be used for dissection by the medical students. In the course of the dissection one of the students found a small metal disk reading SMITH DEAD LIES STILL.

Subsequent investigation revealed that some nine years earlier Jones had had the disk inserted in the flesh of his buttock, confident that dissection would reveal it, thus giving him the last word.

PICTURES OF THE INVISIBLE

A man sent to India to take over the management of a business promised himself that he would personally investigate and endeavor to establish the truth or falsity of the oft-told Indian rope-trick.

When his business affairs in India were under good control, the man began his exhaustive investigation. Finally he was referred to a venerable fakir who purportedly performed the rope-trick and would do so for a proper consideration. The businessman completed arrangements, including agreement that other people should be present at the demonstration.

The businessman, several friends and a professional photographer went to the appointed place—a clearing in the jungle. The wrinkled fakir—a man with strange eyes—had preceded them and was accompanied by a wan little boy with a basket.

The visitors were tense and uneasy. The photographer set up his camera. The others watched every move of the fakir as he made his preparations. They were looking for anything smacking of theatrical hocus-pocus or sleight-of-hand.

The fakir took the basket from the boy, removed from it a knife and a rope. He threw the rope into the air where it immediately became as rigid and straight as a flag pole. At the fakir's order, the boy climbed the rope hand over hand until he was well above the heads of the spectators. The fakir then placed the knife in this teeth and climbed the rope until he had reached the boy. Suddenly and without ceremony the fakir calmly cut off the child's head, threw it to the ground and the boy's body after it. He then slid down the rope, picked up the head and attached it to the body. The boy jumped to his feet and scampered into the surrounding wilderness. The fakir slowly pulled the rope down and called out for the child who diffidently reappeared. The fakir and the child smiled gently, accepted the promised pay and quickly went on their way. The photographer, still gasping with amazement at what he had witnessed and photographed, realized he was the first man to capture on film the famous rope trick. He rushed to get his pictures developed.

The prints were clear and good, but the photographer was aghast. There were pictures of the spectators looking incredulously into the sky—at nothing. There were pictures of them looking down at the ground—horror written on their faces. But in every picture the fakir was standing at the same place on the ground, with the rope in his hand and the little boy standing obediently next to him.

THE CLEVER CABMAN

One day Sir Arthur Conan Doyle arrived in Paris and asked a cab driver to take him to a certain hotel. The cab driver, recognizing his passenger as the famous creator of Sherlock Holmes, said "I perceive, sir, that you have recently visited Constantinople, and there are strong indications you have been in the neighborhood of Milan. I further deduce that you have recently been in Buda."

"Wonderful! Very clever! I'll give you five francs extra if you tell me how you arrived at so accurate a conclusion," said the great author of detective fiction.

"It was easy," said the cab driver proudly. "I simply looked at the labels on your baggage."

LUCK OF THE IRISH

Each year Pat, an elevator operator, faithfully bought a $2.00 Irish Sweepstakes ticket. And each year Pat gave the ticket to his wife

Nora and said, "Don't lose it. This is our year." The indulgent wife smiled tolerantly and said nothing.

Shortly after one of these annual domestic rituals, Nora was shopping at the neighborhood grocery store owned by their good friend Moriarity when it occurred to her to barter the ticket for two dollars worth of groceries. "Pat will never know," she assured herself, "because we haven't a chance of winning." Moriarity accepted the ticket in lieu of money.

When the sweepstakes numbers were drawn, the ticket Pat bought was among them. "Guard that ticket with your life, Nora" he said to his grim-lipped and nervous spouse.

The day of the race Pat and Nora listened tensely for the radio report of the race results—he confident and excited, she fearful and close to hysteria.

Finally the flash came—Pat's horse had won! Wild with joy, Pat leaped to his feet and held his winning ticket aloft as though thousands were watching him. Neighbors rushed in and for a few seconds no one noticed that Nora had fainted.

When Nora was revived a few minutes later her first words were: "Pat—the ticket—how did you get it?"

"Maybe I should have told you I won it back from Moriarity in a poker game several days after you sold it to him. But I wanted to teach you to have faith in my Irish luck."